The True Diaries of a 1970's Teenager

Book 1:

1976

Published By Karen Francis

Copyright © 2024 All Rights Reserved.

No part of this publication may be reproduced, distributed, or transmitted in any form or by any means, including photocopying, recording, or other electronic or mechanical methods, without the prior written permission of the Author.

Karen Francis

For Lizzie

Table of Contents

The True Diaries of a 1970's Teenager 1

Preface 4

The 1970s 7
- Too Many Joe's 8
- The Menagerie 9

1975 13
- Down t'Field 13

1976 17
- First Loves 19

Postscript 80
- Links 81

Preface

I was born in the Swinging '60s, to working-class parents in Nottingham, England. My teenage years were lived during the heady 1970s. If I had to characterise this magical decade it would be with Bellbottom trousers, Glam Rock, Jackie magazine, Space Hoppers, Etch-a-Sketch, platform shoes, power cuts and Clackers (known to us as 'ker-knockers'). I remember the big bruises we had on our arms from banging these glass balls on string together. We tried to minimise the damage by wrapping corrugated cardboard around them - no wonder Clackers were banned.

I kept a daily diary from the age of 14 (1975), until I was 27 (1988) – just before I went off to university as a mature student. I've never read these diaries in any detail until now, as I transcribe the first two of them here (the very end of 1975 and 1976). These tattered books, some written in the tiniest, faded writing, have lived in a box of mementoes, moving with me throughout my life, from country to country and town to town. Knowing what I know now, about the way my life has unfolded, to me they are nostalgic, funny and informative. If you've ever wondered what the '70s

The True Diaries of a 1970's Teenager: 1976

were like for a young teenager, or are perhaps of the same era, join me on this trip down memory lane, back to a time of freedom and teenage innocence, lived during 1976 - a year of social upheaval and a rare British heatwave.

My earliest childhood memories are a series of evocative snapshots: sitting on my grandad's knee on a red tartan blanket; making mud pies in the back porch; meeting Mum on a zebra crossing in an unknown place, a few months after she'd left us; and being held down on a hospital trolley by a big male nurse, while my three partially severed fingers were stitched back together.

I was shy as a child - I remember leaving the Brownie Guides because I was too scared to walk around the giant toadstool to achieve my Promise Badge. By the time I was 8 (in 1969), I had a burning urge to change my Christian name to something more exotic, such as Fern or Cherry. The latter was inspired by cheeky Cherry, the most beautiful (I thought), of the Pan's People dance troop, seen every Thursday night on Top of the Pops – though I seem to remember that my dad preferred the blonde one. My other alternative name choice was 'Billy', after the funny tomboy from my favourite kid's TV show, Double Deckers. The catchy theme tune, 'Get on board, get on board, get on board with the Double Deckers.....' still clear in my mind, all these years later.

For me though, life did not take place, in the words of the song, 'on a Double-decker London bus', but rather on and around the back garden of 20, Springfield Road, Hucknall. This was on a typical 1950s suburban estate in the rural Nottinghamshire Coalfields - Pit Country (just think D.H. Lawrence). The fields and woodlands of my childhood were to play a major part in the development of my character and interests, more than I could have ever imagined: the earth, rocks and broken pieces of pottery I found fuelled my love of all things old and interesting from an early age. Little did I know that the hours spent pacing up and down the nearby ploughed fields, collecting broken pottery sherds, old glass bottles and clay tobacco-pipe stems would lead to an interesting career in archaeology – but that's for another book.

The 1970s

Many of my 1970s teenage memories are naturally clothes-related: proudly getting my first circle skirt that skimmed the top of my black Barter shoes, sweeping the floor as I walked. A Northern Soul-style spin on the Miner's Welfare dance floor gave a spectacular effect. I also recall my floor-length, light grey, leather Gestapo-style coat bought on the market; and my pin-striped trousers or 'Bags' with a wide, 3-button waistband. These were teamed (stylishly), with a Ben Sherman or Simon Shirt with button-down pointy collars. The outfit was completed with a jumper with a stripey waistband and three stars on. Also fashionable were cheesecloth shirts and peasant tops. Another milestone moment was getting my first pair of 4-inch black wedge shoes that rocked like boats when you walked (*'you'll break your neck,'* Dad said).

Later random snapshot memories from the late '70s include buying my first 45 rpm chart single- a difficult choice between David Essex's Lamplight and the popular Monster Mash (no guesses...). I also remember going down the kid's slide in the park, in my new trendy blue mac - whizzing right through a pile of stinking dog muck, cruelly placed there by other bored teenagers.

Too Many Joe's

One of my earliest memories is me trying to cover my ears to the sound of Mum and Dad fighting downstairs – both astrological Scorpios, their jealous stings often clashed and Mum took off a couple of times before leaving for good when I was about 5. Dad had his hands full then, with me and my younger sister Helen fighting like the proverbial cat-and-dog. Dad would try to try to separate us by slapping us pathetically, leaving us both in fits of stifled laughter from his gentle swipes– he was much too kind for discipline.   ʻ

Mum hadn't wanted to move away from her roots in Nottingham City to the small colliery town of Hucknall (pronounced *'ucknall*), where folks talked funny but Dad had insisted, '*It would be good for the kids Sheila, nice schools, lots of fields to play in.*'

Little did he know that a couple of years later, she'd be off up north with 'that Irish fella off the motorway', leaving him to cope with a pair of good, but slightly wild, teenage girls and their ever-growing collection of pets. Sadly, research for this book has suggested that we may have moved away from the City after a neighbour's child (who I should have been staying with), was murdered.

The Menagerie

The upside of Mum leaving is that us two girls were free to the point of feral, filling the house and garden with our beloved animals. At one time, these included gerbils, hamsters, guinea-pigs, 25 rabbits, two cats (Sooty and Twinkle), two dogs (Willy and Nugget), two rescued chickens (Pete and Chippy), a jackdaw and even a pit-pony (Bestwood Joe). I played mostly barefoot in the garden and grew giant vegetables.

One day Dad told us about some fox cubs that a man at work at the Council Depot had saved. 'Dad, can we have one?' we pleaded, 'We can train it like a dog and it can guard the back garden.' Me and 'Our Helen' were so excited about getting the fox cub that we must have 'blabbed' about it to the neighbours. Before we knew it, Mr Willows from across the road had asked Dad to put a stop to our foxy plans. He had a pigeon coop and was worried that the fox would get a taste for the boring birds.

As consolation, Dad bought us an antique stuffed fox in a glass-fronted case. I accidently broke the glass with a hand brush one day while cleaning the floor. This turned out to be a bonus, as we were then able to stroke the fox -and the little Jack Russell dog that was in the case.

A few months after the fox-cub disappointment, a friend's dad had bred some lovely Springer Spaniel-cross pups that were ready to be homed. Three of the pups were brown and white –or 'liver' and white, as I was proud to explain. But there was also a black and white one. It was a dog pup, very cute with spotty legs and big black splodges on his back.

After the constant moaning from us about the fox cub, Dad didn't dare say no to the pup and so 'Willy' arrived. The name was chosen in adoration of a Great Dane (dog) I met with the same name (Pedigree name, Knight's Gift). However, as a teenage girl, I soon found this to be a big mistake. The untrained dog ran off all the time, and it was very embarrassing to have to call 'Willyyy' out loud in the street.

Willy wasn't the only problem animal we had... One day Mrs Westaby from next door banged madly on the back door, *'That bird of yours will be the death of me,'* she screamed, *'it's been chasing me down the path and pecking at my varicose veins. Look at it swinging on my washing line.'* Our Helen was quick to retort, *'Where do you think it's from, Billy Smart's Circus?'* *'Don't you be cheeky you,'* Mrs Westaby snapped, *'or I'll tell your Dad when he comes home. It's not right letting that thing run wild, terrorising everybody.'*

The naughty bird in question was our Freddie, a young mischievous jackdaw named after the strutting Freddie Mercury of Queen, my favourite band at the time. The bird had been found in the woods near the M1 motorway by Craig [Cameron] the budding (and oh so handsome), birdwatcher who lived round the corner. It was true that Freddie was a handful. He slept in one of my rabbit hutches at night, but every morning at the crack of dawn he came tapping on my bedroom window and poking his beaky, grey-capped head through the little hole in the corner of the glass pane, *'Come on, come on, No, No!'* he'd squawk, until I woke up and gave him his breakfast of worms, milk and soggy Weetabix.

Mum came back to live with us briefly when I was 12 or 13, complete with a new half-brother Joe, who we referred to as 'Joe-Jo.' This was so as not to confuse him with his Irish Dad, Big Joe (who sometimes stayed with Dad and us, to the amazement of the neighbours); or with my pit pony, who was also called...Joe.

Karen & Joe-Jo in 1976, with Willy the dog & Sooty the cat

1975

Down t'Field

This was a term of endearment used for the smallholding owned by my horse-owning friends, the Delaney's, who lived round the corner from us and had about 5-acres of land. The head of the family was Jed, a lovely big farmer with a great sense of humour; and his eternally young wife Maureen who, I remember hearing, had a 17-inch waist when they met (and still looks incredible at 87!). I spent every waking hour I could down t'field, or on adventures with the two older sisters Sally and Scarlett.

Jed's oldest daughter Sally was an adventurous, artistic, plucky girl with silken, golden hair and trademark jeans. Besides horsey topics (especially Arabians), Sally's favourite hobbies were listening to the Osmonds (she drooled over Alan, the boring Senior Osmond, while my fave was cheeky chipmunk Merrill). She taught me how to make those classic, 1970s nail-and-string pictures (usually of ships or Spirograph-type circles). Sally also introduced me to the huge Great Danes she worked with (including Knight's Gift, aka Willy), at the local breeding kennels.

One snowy, winter morning Sally knocked on our door and told me she was going up to the plantations near the M1 Motorway to look for animal tracks in the snow. Half an hour later we set off together, armed with crisps, Kit-Kats and Dandelion and Burdock pop. We also had Plaster of Paris to preserve the animal footprints for scientific reasons.

Following a heavy snowfall, during which time we sheltered in the deer lookout, we were very late home. I remember ending the day standing in a washing-up bowl of hot water, in tears, after being heavily chastised by mum, who had been worried sick.

The second oldest Delaney sister, Scarlett was a statuesque, mini-skirted blonde and a legend in the school's Sixth Form. Clever, funny and independent, she was admired by boys, girls and teachers alike. By day, Scarlett could solve a logarithm in seconds and throw a javelin to the end of the sports field. After school, she would appear looking sexy (so the boys said), in a pair of jodhpurs and rubber wellies, and create a stack of heavy hay-bales with a pitchfork in time for tea. She hasn't changed...

The True Diaries of a 1970's Teenager: 1976

Although it seems unlikely that most of the people I once knew will read this book, the names of some folks have been changed or abbreviated for anonymity. To those whose names have not been changed (particularly school friends mentioned briefly), I hope that no-one is offended by being included, but rather, enjoys these memories going back almost 50 years. All of my diary entries and character descriptions are authentic and are reproduced exactly (including their spelling mistakes!), for authenticity. My teenage diary entries begin at the end of 1975:

Sat Dec 27 1975: *Went to see Jaws with Julie W, Sally, Scarlett. Jaws was great.*

It's funny how, even though this was almost 50 years ago, I remember that we went by bus to a distant (for us) cinema in Basford to see this new film. I also remember how everyone in the cinema (including me) stood up and screamed like crazy, when the head fell out of the boat hull!

Sun Dec 28 1975: *Can't remember doing anything but Helen saw me & Sally going down the street. I don't know where I'd been* [good start!].

Mon Dec 29 1975: *Went to cave in morning with EC* [Emma Cameron] *& Helen. Helen & EC went swimming after but I stayed in with Mum & Joe & we watched tele.*

Tue Dec 30 1975: *Went to flicks to see 'Land that Time Forgot.' It was chronic. Went with Helen, EC, RG, JA & Joe. Roxy didn't give us a lift in her van.*

Weds Dec 31 1975: *It rained this afternoon. Went to EC till 11pm. I decided to buy Grub* [guinea pig]. *Craig was mixing drinks up & me & Emma drunk them.*

The True Diaries of a 1970's Teenager: 1976

1976

The following year is recorded in a tiny diary with miniscule writing. It revives wonderful memories of baling hay in the heat of the school summer holidays with the Delaney's.

This was the scorching, crispy summer of 1976, a glorious heatwave. I was almost 15, 'Our Helen' 11. It was a time of freedom and joy for a horse-mad teenage girl, especially when your best friends were Sally and Scarlett. Every day of the school holidays was spent down the field, where the Delaney's kept their horses- Sally's chestnut mare Lady and her foal Flicka; Scarlett's Hunter mare April Star (Lady's first foal); and their dad Jed's Shire horse foal, Misty.

I'd been infected by the 'horse bug' as a result of Black Beauty. Every Sunday night I was reduced to floods of teenage girlie tears, from the sight of the trusty black steed galloping across our TV screen to the heart-wrenching theme tune. 'Dad I want a horse!!', I'd cry and Dad's eyes would roll upwards as he whispered, 'Oh God, not again', through the fumes of his John Player's No. 6 tipped.

Eventually, the weekly grief was more than he could bear. My dreams came true in the form of Bestwood Joe, a 28-year old ex-pit pony, bred from Dartmoor stock and retired from the local colliery after an underground sentence of 14 years pulling coal wagons.

Joe was small and fluffy with sticky-out ribs and knobbly knees from a lifetime of tripping over train tracks, but we loved him. He had the character of a stubborn, grumpy old man, which I suppose he was. He always looked forward to a weekly bucket of pony nuts soaked in stout, which was one of the conditions stipulated, when we adopted him (for free!), from an old ex-miner in the next pit village of Newstead.

Me and Bestwood Joe soon formed a team with cheeky Roxy and her ex-pit pony Stevie, a stocky, stubborn grey Welsh pony. Our romantic dreams of Black Beauty-type canters through leafy woodlands were brought to an abrupt halt on our first outing by the naughty pit-pony collaboration. When we were a few miles away from the yard, the naughty nags bolted on their knobbly knees and dragged us under two, adjacent low branches, knocking us both from their backs. The two equine devils then turned and galloped faster than we had ever seen them, back to their stables for tea, leaving us to trudge the long way back on foot, feeling embarrassed in our grubby jodhpurs, with riding crops in hand.

The 1976 heatwave started in June and lasted for two months. Water was rationed and there were standpipes in the street. As the hot, dry weather continued, the fields and crops were scorched and forest fires broke out. I remember going firefighting one evening with Scarlett in a friend Graham's land rover, batting out flames with branches to help stop the spread of the fire. The month of June also saw our kitchen going up in flames, but that was due to my sister leaving the kettle on the gas stove.

First Loves

As 1976: progresses it becomes clear that at 14, going on 15, I was slowly growing up (we were late developers in the '70s!). Thoughts of horses slowly turned to those of boys. This was the year of first crushes, first kisses and trendy new clothes. Mum got a bar job at the Nabb Inn down the road (affectionately known as something else..), so we often went there.

Thurs 1 Jan 1976: *Bought Grub* [guinea pig] *back but Mum saw it so I took him back again. In afternoon me & Sally walked to kennels but rain made us come back.*

Fri 2 Jan: *Car broke down & me & Helen had to push it to adventure playground. Tonight there was a storm & we had a power cut & we signalled to June & Stan with a torch. I wanted to go down field but Jed said no.*

Sun 4 Jan: *When we all got up today it was 12.00. Today it snowed but melted. Mum's mad cause I got clothes wet. Went to EC's tonight & peeled carrots.*

Tue 6 Jan: *Larry etc wanted me to see Adrian tonight. I know he's ugly really. They are kidding me. Me, JB & Chris laughed at Wiggy cos he was playing Batman.*

Thurs 8 Jan: *I stayed in tonight & watched Top of the Pops. In bed I read Sally's book, The Brumby. It's about a wild horse in Australia.*

Fri 9 Jan: *I went to Sally's tonight & we had a Shandy Mackeson. Went to library tonight because my book* *is overdue. Mum says there is a fine but it is a Junior book.*

Sat 10 Jan: *Went to Delaney's all day & helped Sal do her bedroom. I came home at 11.00 & Mum was mad with me. She said I prefer their house to ours.*

Sun 11 Jan: *Helped Sally do bedroom in morning* [mum's words obviously had no effect]. *Went down field & didn't have dinner. Came home at half past seven.*

Thurs 15 Jan: *I had a scrap with girl at the pub because she threatened me. Me & Rusty played batman for a laugh & we also made a rope swing.*

Sat 17 Jan: *Cleaned shed up, took dog a walk & then went to Scarlett's to see her old bottles. I might go down field in morning.*

Sun 18 Jan: *I overlayed but Scarlett woke me up. We went to see Ni**er then I brushed Misty* [Shire horse foal]. *Stayed at Scarlett's till nine o'clock.*

It's hard to believe, in current times, that we gave the little black Shetland pony this very non-PC name. It was later changed to Sunshine.

Mon 19 Jan: *Didn't go to school because of cookery* [not my favourite subject!]. *Dug garden & then went down field with Scarlett. Started nail picture for Mum* [oh dear, the first of many awful string-picture gifts..].

Tue 20 Jan: *Went down field then I finished my string picture & started another. Came in & watched TV. Big Joe's birthday* [Big Joe was Little Joe's Irish Dad].

Thurs 22 Jan: *Did some gardening & then me & Rusty made some toffee. After we saw Julie & Christine & we all went up to the telephone box.*

Fri 23 Jan: *Me, Chris & Julie went up to phone box & then we had an argument with girls at Nabb Inn. It snowed so we came in. Baby rabbit died.*

Sat 24 Jan: *Snow was thick so me Chris & Julie went sledging. I found Emma's rabbit dead. Tonight I did a jigsaw & watched television.*

Mon 26 Jan: *After school I went down to Nabb & then came in because I didn't feel very well.*

Wed 28 Jan: *Fell out with Rusty cause I promise HG I'd go to her house. At HG's I played chess. I had new trousers, orange ones!*

Thurs 29 Jan: *Watched Top of Pops & then went to Scarlett's. Came back at 11 o'clock. Dad came in & he was drunk.*

Fri 30 Jan: *Cleaned rabbits out & 2 babies had died. Got* [stole!] *food from cabbage field. Came home & had some chips. JA slept at our house.*

As January ends, I am a bit disturbed (in retrospect) by the number of rabbits dying. I also feel compelled to confess that we really did go to the phone box up the street to mess about and make prank calls (the shame). As I recall, there wasn't a lot for 15-year olds to do after school in a rural suburb, apart from doing jigsaws, playing chess, stealing cabbages for the rabbits, going to the tropical fish club and making nail-and-string pictures. As the month's progress it also becomes clear that I virtually lived on chips! I must have been malnourished as a result. It wasn't easy for Dad though, bringing up two teenage girls on his own and feeding them - especially when we had a convenient chippy at the top of our street.

Mon 2 Feb: *After school I mucked about. I saw Sally. She said that Stuart had phoned her.*

Tue 3 Feb: *My Sailfin & my Tetra* [fish] *died. Went to Sally's. Then I watched a very good play about a girl who got murdered.*

Thurs 5 Feb: *Me & Rusty phoned Spud up. Then we saw Moira Jepson & Johnny Jungle carrying on. I came in & watched tele after.*

Fri 6 Feb: *Sold 4 rabbits to pet shop. Tonight I went to beer-off for sweets but they were shut so I went down town on bus instead!*

Sat 7 Feb: *Didn't do much. Scarlett came round & watched two films. Joe bought us some chips.*

Sun 8 Feb: *Tabby didn't have babies so I mated her again. I went a walk with mum & Joe. Stayed in tonight & washed my hair & had a bath.*

The True Diaries of a 1970's Teenager: 1976

Tue 10 Feb: *Stayed in because there was nothing to do because everyone was out.*

Wed 11 Feb: *I was going to sell Tabby but I didn't because I think she might have babies.*

Sat 14 Feb: *Didn't get any Valentines. I went riding with Rusty. It was a good ride.*

Sun 15 Feb: *Went a long walk with big Joe. We saw about 30 deer & Willie chased two red hares.*

Wed 18 Feb: *I burnt Helen's sock on the fire. Went to cave & took soup & food. Me, Rusty & Roxy & Helen went.*

Thurs 19 Feb: *Big Joe went back today. I miss going a walk. Today I had nothing to do.*

Fri 20 Feb: *I ordered a new dress out of Rusty's catalogue. I planted seed potatoes & then went to a bottle dump at Grannies- got a little brown one.*

Sat 21 Feb: *Did garden at the top. Tonight Scarlett came round for a while. We had some chips.*

Sun 22 Feb: Did garden again. Delaney's went to see Quality Fair the stallion.

Wed 25 Feb: Went to Padstow disco. A lad asked me to go out with him but I said no he was [crossed out] called Terry.

Fri 27 Feb: I took dog walk up Rocks & looked for bottles on the cornfield. Came in & watched TV.

Sun 29 Feb: Played tennis with RG, HG & their dad. I stayed at their house until 10.00. We were drinking sherry.

Mon 1 Mar: My new pink dress arrived today. Mum didn't like it all that much.

Tue 2 Mar: Roxy's dad insulted Helen so we went to play tennis with JA. We watched David Delaney having a scrap.

Fri 5 Mar: I gave Roxy a mouthful for spreading roumers [sic]. After me & Emma Cameron made some toffee. It was lovely.

The True Diaries of a 1970's Teenager: 1976

Mon 8 Mar: Had day off school & dug all blackcurrants up & gave them to Scarlett.

Wed 10 Mar: Tabby had 8 babies. Tonight I had play rehearsal & did my art after.

Fri 12 Mar: Stayed in all night. The horror film was Dracula. It was old & a load of rubbish.

Sat 13 Mar: Grub has had three babies. Me & Emma Cameron made some fudge tonight.

Sun 14 Mar: Cleaned shed out & then went a walk with EC & her dad. I had two guppies & 1 died.

Mon 15 Mar: Had a play rehearsal until 7.00. Came straight in & went to bed.

Tue 16 Mar: Had a play rehearsal. Scarlett wanted me to foster 8 baby rabbits but I said we've already got 8.

Wed 17 Mar: We went all the way through the play, the Sgt Major is really funny. We were in hysterics.

Thurs 18 Mar: *Helen, EC, RG, Kit, Karen, Copo, Benny & loads more came to see play. They seemed to enjoy it. We did.*

The school play, about football supporters, was after the 1967 production Zigger Zagger, by Peter Terson.

Fri 19 Mar: *After the play Scarlett came to watch horror film about a meteorite. I've seen it before, it makes things grow massive.*

Sat 20 Mar: *Play was best night yet. I went to the party after. I fell down & grazed me badly.*

Sun 21 Mar: *Mum had to go to the hospital. So did June in same ward with same trouble! & same day.*

Mon 22 Mar: *Had day off to look after Joe-Jo. We went to see Mum & June tonight.*

Tue 23 Mar: *Went to see Mum. June had had her appendix out. Mum says she will be home tomorrow. Had day off.*

Wed 24: *Mum came home. I stayed off again.*

The True Diaries of a 1970's Teenager: 1976

Thurs 25 Mar: *Had day off & I mended back of shed. Went & played cards at Delaney.*

Fri 26 Mar: *Went to Hucknall Market & got Mum a Mother's Day pressie. I saw Larry on the market getting a leather jacket.*

Sat 27 Mar: *Went to jumble sale & then went to collect bottles with Emma W. Only me got one, it's a good one. She saw it first, picked it up said, 'uh rubbish' & chucked it down again.*

Sun 28 Mar: *Mothering Sunday I gave her a jug & then did some gardening.*

Mon 29 Mar: *Made Floppy a new hutch & stayed in when it was finished.*

Thurs 1 Apr: *Went to Hazel Grove disco. At school we played tricks on Knotty & Mrs Reeves.*

Sat 3 Apr: *Finished library book. I cried. Saw Euro Song Contest & Grand National on TV. I wrote to Karin Koll in Germany. Then I lent Sally my library book.*

Sun 4 Apr: *Cleared shed up & put windows in it. Had a fire, collected rabbit food & some plastic for frames.*

Mon 5 Apr: *Collected rabbit food & tidied shed up ready for school guinea pigs. Made lettuce frames.*

Tue 6 Apr: *Larry & co came for me but I was out getting a rat-trap from EC for the shed.*

Thurs 8 Apr: *Dug garden & then went down field & brushed Misty. I came home at nine o'clock. Scarlett showed me her fossils from Geog trip.*

Fri 9 Apr: *Mr Knott left our school. We bought him some daffodils. We broke up for two weeks. I dug all the garden tonight.*

Sat 10 Apr: *I did some gardening & then me & EC tried to sell some old bottles at an antique shop. Then me & Rusty made some jam tarts & ginger beer.*

Sun 11 Apr: *Went up Rocks a bit & then went & caught 2 frogs with EC in afternoon. Later I went for catkins with HG. Went to EC & made plaster casts of*

Brandy's paws. Had a clay lobbing battle & then made fudge.

Mon 12 Apr: Got up at 12.00 & went up brickyard with EC. We got some frog spawn. After a man bought a baby rabbit & then Sally came round all night.

Tue 13 Apr: Went to HGs till 6.00. Came home & had high-fin swordtail fish. Then the two horses up Misk got out & me, Sal, Helen & June took them back. I came in & watched The Evacuees.

Wed 14 Apr: Took typewriter to be mended. Went to pet shop & had a Mollie. After I went a walk with Sally & EC & we got lost & ended up in Moorgreen. We walked all the way home! Helen got me an angel from fish club.

Thurs 15 Apr: Got some frogsporn [sic], sold the brown baby rabbit & then I went to see if B Joe was coming at 9.00. He came at 10.30.

Sat 17 Apr: Sold 4 rabbits & 2 guinea pigs to pet shop. I got £1.80 for them. Now I've got £2.16p for my typewriter. Tonight thriller was very good.

Mon 19 Apr: At 2.00 we all went to Wollaton Hall. We got back at 6.30 & all stayed in. At W.H. Dad pulled a girl's hair off with his button.

Tue 20 Apr: Stayed in this morning & we all went to Newstead Abby in the afternoon. Had arguement [sic] with Mum so we're not talking. At N.A. a boy nearly drowned.

Wed 21 Apr: Joe went back today. Me & Dad went with him to station. We saw a puff with rings on. After me & Dad went to Victoria Centre. Then I made some cloches.

Thurs 22 Apr: Made a new back for the shed, smashed tabbies hutch up & put her in with the guinea-pigs. Later I went to rope swing but I had to come back because my foot was hurting (I trod on a nail).

Fri 23 Apr: Went to Newstead Abby with Stan, June & Helen. We met Craig Cameron & his mates there. They went in late for swan's eggs & we got some oysters. Tonight I went to Sally's.

The True Diaries of a 1970's Teenager: 1976

Sat 24 Apr: Went to Scarlett's Uncle Harry's & her Mamma's as well. After, me & Sally went to farmhouse for things. Craig was there already. He shouted 'Oi' & scared me to death. After I stood & talked to him a bit. Stan cut his tendon today.

Mon 26 Apr: School again! Chippy opened up, up the street. Mum smacked me up so I went out. I got fish cake & chips for 10p.

Tue 27 Apr: Something terrible had happened this morning - the school guinea pig had gone. I told Mr Whitehead. All he said was 'Blast' & told me not to worry. Tonight I got a black eye. Got school guinea pig back.

Wed 28 Apr: Sold a baby rabbit to Liz O'Sullivan. Tonight me & Stan & Helen & June went to fish club. I won perfume on the raffle. A taxidermist from Wollaton Hall gave a talk.

Thurs 29 Apr: Went to funeral directors [no idea why] & then went to orchard & saw Sally & had some chips. Came in & watched TV until 11.30 & went to bed. Flemish making a nest [this likely meant that the poor rabbit was pregnant again].

Fri 30 Apr: *got 200 lines off Lowe did them & then went to HG's to see if she is going for some Barters [70's shoes] with me tomorrow. I watched Freddie Star on TV. He was very good. After I watched film.*

Sat 1 May: *Went down Notts with HG for some Barters. After I watched Southampton win FA Cup. It was a good match. I feel sorry for Man United. After I watched the television.*

Sun 2 May: *CL20: dress half paid for. In morning I went a walk up Misk. Helen's ball got stuck in a tree because I kićked it. After me & EC went a walk up Misk & Brickyard. Willie killed a rat. Tonight Moby Dick was on TV.*

Mon 3 May: *After school I cleaned rabbits out & went for EC to see about selling Flemish but she wasn't in so I came in & had chips & then I didn't feel very well so I went to bed early.*

Tue 4 May: *Had day off because I wasn't very well. Made a nice cake but Mum dropped it. Later on I went up brickyard & got some wood with Stan & June. Stopped in after.*

Wed 5 May: After school I made a frame for cucumbers & then me Rox & Helen went up brick yard & got about £5.00 worth of Trevira each. A man told us to clear off so we ran. After I saw a good play on TV.

The disused brickyard was across the fields from us. A Sunday market was held there and lots of stuff was left behind by traders, so we used to walk there and see what we could find.

Thurs 6 May: Went & dumped a load of junk up back lane with June & Emma C. When I came in I did some H/wk & watched a program about David Bowie on TV. Then I had some pop & chips. Went to bed at 11.00.

Sat 8 May: At 2.30 I went to Geoff's wedding. Got back at 11.30. We had a great time. This morning Zak & her 6 babies had got out. We only found five babies. Had some chips when we got back.

Sun 9 May: There's still no sign of Zaks baby. Today I got rabbit food & then went down to the barn with Julie & Christine.

Mon 10 May: Tonight I tidied some of the garden & planted some seeds. Then me & EC & Billy went a walk & a horse chased Billy. Then at 9.30 I dumped some rubbish & then stayed in.

Tue 11 May: Collected some hay & cleaned shed up. Hoed garden. Saw June & then went to Sally's to get Gt Dane addresses for Spud. Came in & watched a good play about a man that beat his kid up. Then I saw Chris, Brasso & Colly in chip shop.

Thurs. 13 May: Flemish had one baby today. After school I iced Joe's birthday cake & then went to school disco. We went up 6 form base & listened to heavy music. The school disco was crap.

Fri 14 May: Flemish's baby died. After school I went down town for Joe's presents then I had to make sausage rolls. At 7.30 I went a long walk near Rocks & got some chickweed. When I got back Flemish had had some more babies.

Sat 15 May: It was Joe's birthday. He had a wigwam. I stayed in all day & got his party ready. After I watched TV about until about 11.45 then went to bed cause I was very tired & I couldn't keep my eyes open.

Mon 17 May: Tonight me, EC, Helen & AR went to brickyard & got 200 pencils. Then a man chased us (Harvey's dad). Then me & AR saw a cyst on the little white rabbit.

Thurs 20 May: Had day off & me & Mum put my Trevira jacket together, did bedrooms for Mum, earthed tatties up & went up Rocks with dog. Came in at 9.15. Wrote a poem, had chips & watched a terrible film.

Fri 21 May: Had day off school. Mum made me a Trevira jacket. Later I went to Scarlett's then came home & played records. At 11.00 a film was on but it was rubbish so I went to bed.

Sun 23 May: I saw an adder in the orchard about 2ft away. At 9.00 I went down field. Me, Sal, Scar & Graham went to Sue H's. Then I had dinner & me, Sal, Janie & Jed went down field. Car fell on Jed. Later me & Sal got an evening job for £2.25. [I think this was for the whole job posting 1000's of leaflets!].

Tue 25 May: Did some leaflets on Long Hill Rise. It rained & I got soaked. We came in at 9.00 again. There wasn't anything good on TV so I went to bed.

Wed 26 May: Paid FC membership. Had Rounders match. After it was fish club show. I didn't get anything Sally got 2nd with a fighter [Siamese Fighting fish].

Thurs 27 May: Flemish babies opened their eyes today. Finished the leaflets off with Rusty & EC. Got in at 10.00 & had to make a house for RE.

Fri 28 May: After school I planted some seeds. Then I had some chips. At 6.30 Big Joe came. Me & Helen camped out. My feet were freezing so I might not camp out again.

Sat 29 May: Went to pet shop but came back because the girl turned up. After I got 50p for doing the kitchen. Later on I strung the beans up & at 9 o'clock I started to dig the bushes up at the side of the fence. Two baby rabbits died today.

The True Diaries of a 1970's Teenager: 1976

Sun 30 May: Didn't do much this morning but tonight me & June camped out on her garden. It was great fun apart from my feet being cold.

Mon 31 May: Stopped at June's nearly all day. We camped out. At 12 we had some porridge - at 2.00 am we walked up road to CW's.

Tue 1 June: In the morning I sold 3 rabbits & a guinea pig to the pet shop. In afternoon Dad had to go to the hospital. Mum went with him.

Wed 2 May: Stopped in this morning. In the afternoon I went to see Dad. After I played records. Then I went to Sally's & we were all trying to make Sally put a skirt on.

Thurs 3 June: Stopped at home all day. I cleared garden & shed up. At 7.00 I did front garden. After I had a fire & burnt the trees (Mum went to see Dad this afternoon).

Fri 4 June: This morning I got a cheese cloth off the market. I painted the porch & loo when I got back. Later I went to Scar's & met Michael (Her Boyfriend) came in & watched a film.

I clearly remember that I re-painted our brick porch and loo walls in a vibrant purple colour – very 70s. This part of our house is etched in my memory, as Dad later collapsed in the purple loo, prior to passing away in an ambulance outside.

Sat 5 June: *Didn't wake up till 2.00. At 7.00 I went to see Dad. I got back at 9.30. I stopped in & watched a horror story. It was very good. It was about a Pentacle & a boy possessed by the Devil.*

Tue 8 June: *Julie Robinson wants rabbit. At 6.00 Vera came & ordered 2 grey ones. Then me & Sal took a cockerel up the field. When I got in a good program was on about the Loch Ness Monster.*

Wed 9 June: *After school me & Rusty messed about & then made coffee fudge. After we flew our kites. They went up high becos [sic] there was a very big wind.*

Thurs 10 June: *Went a walk up Misk. Came in & watched Top of the Pops, Porridge & Monty Python, went on garden & watered veg & then came in & saw Police Story.*

The True Diaries of a 1970's Teenager: 1976

Fri 11 June: *I went up Misk hills with Helen & I flew Joe's kite. Later Dad phoned from Derby Infirmary & we were talking for ages. I think I'm going to cattle market tomorrow.*

Sat 12 June: *This morning me & Helen went to cattle market. Got £1.90 for rabbits but bought 3 hens. On way back I saw Mike. Tonight I was going to go to JS house but I stopped at home. Finished the run for the chickens.*

Sun 13 June: *This morning I finished the run off. I didn't have any dinner. This afternoon I watched World at War. Later I spoke to EC, RG & Helen. When I came in a good film was on.*

Tue 15 June: *I went down the field again & when we got back we arranged about going to Arab horse show. I came in & watered the veg then I went to the shop. There wasn't much on TV so I went to bed after I had done my art exam (piccy of the dog).*

Wed 16 June: *When I got home I went to Waddo's for a bale with JA. After I cleaned chickens out & then helped June on her garden. I came in & saw the*

Survivors & then stopped June's till 10.00. SW wants to go out with Andy.

Thurs 17 June: *Bought Julie's dress off her. I stopped in & watched Top of the Pops. Then I went to HG's until about 9.15. When I came in I saw a program about witches & wrote an essay for H/wk.*

Fri 18 June: *Tonight I sorted some old books out & then collected some rabbit greens. Sally came round so we went to her house & Michael (Scar's boyfriend was there so I stayed & talked to him).*

Sat 19 June: *Got up at 10.00. Did some gardening. At 2.00 me & Helen went to see Dad. He's at the City hospital now & he looks much better. When I came back I went to Scarlett's house. Me & Sally went to our friend Jennie's house for an hour. Then I saw Clint Walker film.*

Sun 20 June: *This morning I sold two baby rabbits to Vera. Got back at 12.30 had dinner & went to EC's. We went to see some Springer pups- £250. After me & EC got some leaflets off the woman on Polperro Way. When I got home Helen had set the kitchen on* *fire. 8 panes of glass are broke, wires are burnt, ceiling's burnt, curtains burnt (in fire).*

I remember there were hordes of people on our back garden looking at our burnt kitchen/ conservatory. Mum came home and, obviously horrified, shouted, 'Thank you for your help- ALL of you!' The crowd dispersed.

Mon 21 June: *At 5.00, me & EC did 600 leaflets. When we finished it was 8.00. I came in. Later Sally came round with some stuff for the chickens. At 9.00 I had a bath & then went to bed & revised Chem for exams.*

Tue 22 June: *Didn't do any leaflets. Went to see EC's Springer pup & then went a walk up Misk. At 6.00 <u>Dad came back from hospital.</u> At 8.00 I did some weeding. Watched TV at 9.00 about farm animals & then revised in bed.*

Thurs 24 June: *Sally came round at 11.00 cos she'd had an argument. Had detto [detention?] till 4.30. At 5.00 me & EC did 600 leaflets up Ruffs Estate. When I got in I went to bed & revised Chem because exams are next Wed Thurs & Fri.*

Fri 25 June: *Didn't do much at school cos it was too hot. Tonight I did some leaflets (last 200) & then went to the Secondary Summer Fete. At about 11.00 Big Joe came with some strawberries.*

Sat 26 June: *Got up at 9.00 went for my wages from leaflets but didn't get them. After I sold two baby rabbits to the pet shop for 70p. At 8.30 Rusty & EC came for me. Went in at 10.00 & got in a cold bath. I can't get to sleep now because it's too hot (going to seaside tomorrow).*

Sun 27th June: *Day Trip to* [crossed out- Skegness?] *Seaside. Had a good day out. I got a photo album & a cheesecloth what was £1. Went in the sea. It was lovely! On the way back on the bus I was sick. We stopped at a pub & Mum was there.*

Mon 28 June: *School again! Tonight I saw Scarlett & we went baling at Bulwell Hall with Mike (Scar's boyfriend) & Jed. When I came in I revised Chem & Geog. I've got a lovely bruise on my leg from baling!*

Tue 29 June: *EC came for me so gave her her £3.00. We went to PO & then went on her garden. Craig* *wants to do same job as me! Later we went to Renu's house. Then I came in.*

Wed 30 June: *Had exams all day at school. Tonight I've been down field & then revised with Scarlett for two hours (chem). When I came in & did another hour I've now just finished making maths.*

Thurs 1 July: *Had some more exams. Tonight I went to Craig's house & me & Emma helped him do his garden. After we got some strawberries from his Auntie Cath's* [highlighted- this was coded for scrumping..]. *Came in & Dad was in a bad mood.*

Fri 2 July: *Exams have finished at school. At 8.00 me & EC went in her bedroom. After she went in & I went on garden & weeded at the top. Then I saw film about a madhouse but it was crap so I went to bed.*

Sat 3 July: *Got up at 8.30 went to Larry's house & Larry, me, Julie, Andy & Rusty went down Notts. I got a bikini but it's too small so I'm taking it back. Tonight we all went to Dawn's disco. Had a laugh. Then me & Rusty & Brasso had to walk home at 11.30 from Papplewick cos we couldn't get a lift. Was scary going thro [sic] Linby.*

Sun 4 July: I didn't wake up till 12.00. Went for EC, but she was going to the Lido, went for JA, & then RG & Helen came. Me, Sal, RG & JA went down the field & then we went to see True Grit.

Mon 5 July: Me & Sally took Flicka a walk & I saw Sharon Hufton. When we got back up fed her & then we walked home.

Tue 6 July: Me & Sally took Flicka a walk around Shortwood Estate. Flicka kept rearing up in the streets because Lady was shouting her

Wed 7 July: Didn't see Sally because she went to the Fish Club. I stopped in all night because knowone [sic] wanted to come out.

Thurs 8 July: Didn't go to school today because it is Sports Day. Did garden this morning. Saw EC tonight for a bit, & saw Sally came in at 10.

Sat 10 July: At 11.30 I went down Notts with HG for a new bikini. Took other one back & went to Richard Shops. I saw Mark Linford from Padstow down Notts. Got home at 3.00 went down field & to a man's house.

He breeds rabbits & said Floppy can't go in a show because I'm not a member of the Rabbit Association.

Sun 11 July: *Fire over slag heaps burnt 70 acres- we saw it. Jed ploughed round it. Got up at 8.30 & went to Lido in new bikini with Joe, Helen & RG. Christine & JB were there. Helen & RG went home on their own & me & Joe got a lift on Jed's trailer. There was a 70 acre fire.*

Mon 12 July: *Went to school. After I went to Scar's & played draughts & chess with Sally. Came in at 9.30. Rained tonight for first time in weeks. Joe went back today. We won't see him till Christmas.*

Tue 13 July: *Dropped a pint mug through sink today & broke it* [it's unclear which is broken but I think I cracked the sink and that the heavy pint pot survived!].

Fri 16 July: *Tonight I went down field with Scarlett & when we were coming home Kev F asked me to go out with him. I didn't say anything.*

Sat 17 July: *Went down field this morning. Baling tonight. Mark Slater & Stan tried to drag me in their tent but June rescued me.*

Wed 21 July: *Karin Koll* [German penfriend from the Queen Fan Club] *wrote & ses [sic] she can come. Tonight I tried to sell three chickens but I couldn't. Then little Justin cut his head in our yard & I took him home & he had to have 2 stitches.*

Thurs 22 July: *Dress is now paid for. Hooray. I stayed on the garden all night & planted radish, beet & swedes. Came in & watched Olympics. Nadia Comanech [sic] got four 10's. Chicken had died today.*

On July 18, 1976, Nadia Comăneci made history at the Montreal Olympics when she was awarded the first perfect 10 in Olympic gymnastics for her routine on the uneven bars.

Fri 23 July: *Broke up at school. At 6.00 Andy came & told me I could babysit. I went at 8.00 & he came home at 12.45. When I got home I was locked out so I had to go & see Mum at the pub.*

The True Diaries of a 1970's Teenager: 1976

Sat 26 July: *Planted some cabbage. Then I put an advert in P.O. about selling my roller skates. Watched James Bond & then Sally came round.*

Tue 27 July: *Jed has got a broken rib today. It was weak from when the car fell on him (23 May).*

Wed 28 July: *Got up late & went down field. They were combining. Julie W. was supposed to come up but didn't come. We got home at 8.30 & fetched Julie. I came in & got things ready. Went to bed at 10.00.*

Thurs 29 July: *Got up at five because of Peterborough show. At 6.00 I went to Scarlett's at 7.00 we were at the station at 7.45 we were at Grantham at 8.30 we were at the bus station. All office men had been on the Peterborough train. At 9.15 we got to the show. Me, Scarlett & Julie had a great fun. Sue & Sally were being snotty all day. At 6.15 we caught the bus but missed the train & got the 8.30 one & talked to army lads. Got 11.00 train at Grantham.*

More information on this day comes to light in one of my school essays from around the same time. We were sitting in the café, waiting for the train, when Scarlett announced that she'd seen our train getting ready to depart. To get to the right platform, we had to cross over an old wooden bridge. In the panic, I lost my shoe between the wooden slats. As a result, our Scottish friend Haggis got drenched in Sally's pop as she fell forward down the steps. On the train we joked about the bouncing cheese sandwiches and warped chocolate, both courtesy of British Rail.

Sun 1 August: *Got up at 9.00 went down town. Then I went to EC's. Cleaned windows for her mum. She brought us some chips. Then I came home & watched TV.*

Mon 2 August: *(Dad in hospital) Saw EC. She said Craig had shot Brandy last night in her neck. Had my dinner at 3.00 & then played Frustration with Emma in shed.*

Sun 8 August: *Helped Mum this morning. After dinner Mum said me, Rox, Helen & EC could camp out. We had great fun tonight. At 5.00 Dad went back to hospital.*

Mon 9 Aug: *It was cold in tent. Got up at 6.00. We all played scrabble later. I saw Scarlett & we got blackberries. Then B Joe went back. Layed [sic] new* carpet & then Rusty & her French cousin Natalie came for me. We went a walk.

Tue 10 Aug: In morning I went blackberrying with Scarlett. After I saw EC & we went to Lido.

Wed 11 Aug: Went to the Lido with Craig, Stan, Lynda, Emma & Rox. Came home at 5.00. I bussed home. Stayed in tonight.

Thur 12 Aug: Went to Lido at 2.00 with EC, HG & Joe. We met JA, RG & Helen. I dived off the top diving board. We got home at 8.30. Stayed in tonight.

Fri 13 Aug: Saw EC. We've arranged to go to Lido tomorrow. Tonight I went to see Dracula at EC's but TV broke down. Then I had some chips at Betty's house with Mum at 12.00.

Sat 14 Aug: Got up at 8.30 & went to Lido with EC, JA & Helen. Then I had to stay in & look after Joe. When I got back watched two horror films Phantom of Opera & Jekyll & Hyde.

Sun 15 Aug: Southwell Show - went with MR, AR, Scarlett, Jed, Mrs. Delaney, Jimmy dark, kids & Kevin.

Stayed with Scar, AR & MR. We went home at 4.00. After I nicked Sally's jeans & we made SALLY PUT A SKIRT ON & she went to pub (everyone cheered).

Tue 17 Aug: *Went to Lido at 12. Been down field this morning. At Lido I saw Annette. On way home I stopped & saw Mum's house. It's nice. Went to Scar's tonight. Got home at 11.30 & I was locked out.*

Wed 18 Aug: *Mum was down Notts all day. I did garden & later went up Rocks with EC & Rosa. Rosa lives nr Chippenham Rd at Bestwood Pk & knows about the girl who was killed with knife & an iron.*

Chippenham Road (no. 15), was where we lived until I was about 5. I remember being told as a teenager that I was supposed to be sleeping at a friend's house across the road but didn't, and that tragically, she was murdered that same night. A search of the internet has revealed this story to be true: in July 1966, Derrick Lawrence Scott, 21, of 14, Chippenham Road, was jailed for life at Nottinghamshire Assizes, for the murder of 10 year old Catherine Mary O'Gorman on 24 April. He beat her about the head and stabbed her. Mary was found on her the floor of her home with a nine-inch wound.

The True Diaries of a 1970's Teenager: 1976

I was nearly 5 when this happened. This must be why we moved house to Hucknall around that time.

Thur 19 Aug: *This morning I went black berry picking up the Rocks. Got 2lbs. After I went to Mum's house. Got back at 4.40 & watched TV. Tonight I went down town & saw Andy, Larry, Karen Wyng, & Alison Smith. Got back & had chips.*

Fri 20 Aug: *Went down town. Had a new dress. Went on market with Mum. Tonight I went to Larry's & me, Alison, Andy, Larry & Julie went in Julie's house. Had a good time. We played records. Got in at 11.00.*

Sat 21 Aug: *This morning I went down town. Saw Larry & Andy on Market. After I had been home about 1 hr I went down again & got Sally's B.day pressie. Tonight I watched Devil Dolls & Frank's Woman (new version).*

Sun 22 Aug: *S'afternoon I went to Grantham to fetch Scarlett back. On motorway me, Sal & Jed were racing MR & Scar (65mph).*

Mon 23 Aug: *In Notts today there have been 300 fires (record). Me & Scarlett & Graham went fire-fighting in Land Rover. Then went to Graham's till 11.00.*

Tue 24 Aug: *S'afternoon I played Monopoly wif [sic] Lynda & EC. I fell out of game cos I was bankrupt (I'm rubbish at it).*

Wed 25 Aug: *Saw EC in morning. She went to Lido I went to Scar's. Then tonight I played Monopoly with Rosa & EC & then saw It shouldn't happen to a vet.*

Thur 26 Aug: *Mum & Helen went to house s'afternoon. I played Monopoly with EC & Craig. I lost. Then I went to Scarlett's & saw Top of Pops. MR was at Scar's house. Chi-Lites, you don't have to go.*

Fri 27 Aug: *Mum & Helen didn't come back so I did housework all day. At 4.00 Graham came & chopped lilac tree down (Hooray). Then I frizzed my hair & Joe came.*

Sat 28 Aug: *Saw Scarlett this morning. I couldn't show off my hair cos it was raining & I had my anorak & hood on.*

The True Diaries of a 1970's Teenager: 1976

Sun 29 Aug: Tonight I went to the fair near the Forest Hotel. Slept the night at Mums.

Mon 30 Aug: Me, Mum, Joe, Helen & Joe-Jo went to Moorgreen Show. I saw Scarlett & Michael there.

Wed 1 Sept: I made some jam today & then went to Mums at 7.00. Saw On the Buses film.

Thur 2 Sept: Saw two fallow deer today. Got home from Mums at 12.30, cleaned up & watched TV. Dad went out. When he came back he got me some chips.

Fri 3 Sept: Made some bread & then saw EC. Tonight I went babysitting at Andy's got 65p (going tomorrow).

Sat 4 Sept: This morning I went down Notts with our Helen & I got a skirt for school. Went to Andy's from 9.30- 11.30 got 65p! EC went on holiday.

Sun 5 Sept: Tonight me & Sal biked down to Mums but I had a flat so we didn't get there very fast. Got woken up at 11.30. We all went to Mums today & had dinner. I came home with Dad cos we are going out tomorrow. Helen stayed.

Mon 6 Sept: *Didn't go out with Dad. I was dead angry. Well I did go out but when I got there he had lost his cheque so we had to come back.*

Tue 7 Sept: *We tried again today. This time we took the cheque & I had a Simon Shirt for school cos we go back tomorrow.*

Wed 8 Sept: *School again. It was dead good. I got split up & now I sit with four girls from Beardall (one goes out with Brian Willows). Four girls are Gill Kane, Max Thring, Sue Taylor, Lesley Allen.*

Thur 9 Sept: *Had office practice & typing all morning. I hated it. I can't do typing cause of my bad finger. Tonight I went down field. We all went a run to Derby (Me, Kev & Scar & Jed).*

Fri 10 Sept: *At school I told Mr Driver I didn't want to do T & O.P., so he said I can change. Dad got a cheque from pools today! – 10p! He said we won £4,000. Tonight I went babysitting. He forgot to pay me.*

Sat 11 Sept: *Did bedrooms this morning, went down field at 5.00. Got back & went babysitting at Andy's at*

9.00. Got £1.20 for yesterday & today. Got back at 12.30 & saw Dracula on our tele.

Sun 12 Sept: £5.50 saved. Got up at 11.30 saw EC. She gave me some rock from Mablethorpe. Then I went to Mums. I've decided I'm going to save up for a leather jacket. Stayed at Mum's tonight.

Mon 13 Sept: <u>My birthday</u> Had some money- £5 & 4 box of chocs. Sally gave me chocs & £1.00 for a fish (going on Fri). Tonight me & Sandra went on park.

Thur 16 Sept: £6.50 saved for jacket. Went down field tonight then I came in at 8.00. Mormons came to door & asked me if my husband was in. I said No. Then they talked to Dad for 15 minutes. I went to see JB & Chris.

Fri 17 Sept: Babysitting. After school I went down field then went to Andy's. He gave me £1.20. Came home at 10.00 because baby had nightmares & he told me to phone him up if she did.

Sat 18 Sept: Gill's Wedding. Got up at 10.00 left here at 2.00. Got to church, Gill was shaking like a leaf. After reception we had a disco & the record player kept breaking down. Got home at 11.00 in taxi.

Sun 19 Sept: £7.00 saved. Stayed in all morning & made some Cornish pasties for dinner. Then I stayed in till 7.00, went to Scarlett's till 10 then I came home.

Mon 20 Sept: Typing tonight. Went to office practice, it was boring. After I stayed at Mums cause I had argument with Dad.

Tue 21 Sept: Scar's B.D. I forgot to buy her anything. Tonight I went to her house. She was drunk. MR & Mick was there. Then I read Sal's diary from 6 years ago.

Wed 22 Sept: Today at school Graham C. asked me to go out with him. I didn't say anything but Shaz said that I said I'll see.

Thur 23 Sept: I've decided not to have a jacket, I'm going to the Wrangler factory. Tonight I walked home with Gill & Bev. [crossed out] Someone has split Gaz Morton & Bobby up & she is blaming it onto Julie B. Tonight I called at Mums for my coat etc.

Fri 24 Sept: Tonight after school I went to Wrangler shop but I didn't have time to get any jeans. Went in

Land Rover. After I came in & went babysitting at Andy's.

Sat 25 Sept: *Took Jane L's £4.00 back then went to Aiden Randall's house. We had great fun (me & Scar). Aiden's back was hurting. Scarlett & Mike went to a disco. I came home on bus at 8.30. Rox & Helen got on bus at market. Then RG came to our house at 9.30. Slept in shed because I broke glass door tonight.*

I remember that I slammed the door in a temper because I couldn't have any chips from the chippy. To my horror, the big glass pane smashed and I was so scared of the consequences that I ran away. I walked the streets for an hour, then got in Floppy's big rabbit hutch in the shed! Dad found me asleep there at 2am, just as he was about to call the police.

Sun 26 Sept: *This morning I went to Scar's & went down field. MR came up & we went bottle digging up the spinney. I got a poison bottle. Tonight I had a mushroom omelette at HGs.*

Mon 27 Sept: *Typing. At six I went mushroom picking. HG started with me but she went back. I went alone* got about 50 mushrooms. Had day off school. Tonight I saw Scar for 1 hour came in. Had chips.

Tue 28 Sept: Had day off because my cold's just as bad bought Queen's 'Sheer Heart Attack' & a diary with a lock on for next year. Later I went down field after going in Dad's lorry. Tonite I saw TV (Charles Dickens) & had some chips.

Wed 29 Sept: School today? No. Tonight I went to Scarlett's. We fetched Wilma [One of the Delaney's pigs, the other being Wilbur] from the knackers & then Alistair Morton chopped her up. Jed gave me a beautiful joint of pork. Then I had some chips when I came in.

Thur 30 Sept: Had another day off & cooked the belly pork that Scarlett gave me. Wilma was luvly (sorry Wilma). I feel a bit guilty now. Tonight I went babysitting for Andy. Saw Oklahoma.

Sun 3 Oct: I think I've got to go to Mums tomorrow but I might go mushrooming. MR has gone. Got loads of mushrooms, went to Mums, had dinner came back then I saw Scarlett & Annette came for me but she only wants me when she isn't going out so I went in

Scar's. This morning I rode Blue down field. Tonight saw film Summer 43.

Mon 4 Oct: Had OP. After I saw Scarlett. Then EC & me sat & talked. We are going mushroom picking tomorrow at 6.30. Tonight. I saw Sweeney. This morning. I got mushrooms (BIG ones!).

Tue 5 Oct: Didn't get many mushys. Had typing all morning. Had dinner down town. Tonite went to Scar's a while & recited my poem. Then I came in & saw TV. Going to do a string picture for Dad.

Wed 6 Oct: Today I overlaid. Tonight I started a present for Dad's Bday. Then I came in & saw TV (Horse of the Year Show). Debbie Johnsy won. Had chips & then washed hair.

Thur 7 Oct: Need £4, I've got 60p. Goose Fair starts. I'm not going to the fair this year. Today had typing & OP all morning. Bought stuff for Dad's Bday at dinner then saw Sally & came home. Tonight I did some more of Dad's Pressie then saw film on TV. Went to Carol's. Mum came up.

Fri 8 Oct: Today Aiden Randall found out I was called Fifi. I'll never live it down now. Tomorrow he's coming mushroom picking. Tonight I finished Dad's pressie off. It's a nail & thread piccy of a yacht. Tonight I went to Andy's, going tomorrow.

Sat 9 Oct: Went mushroom picking, Aiden didn't come. Me & Scarlett went & got loads of massive ones. Then we biked to his house. He was still in bed! Then I stayed at Scarlett's till 5.00. Then I had a load of chocs. Went babysitting. Andy gave me £1.50. Wrote a poem about Dougall. It's in next year's diary.

Sun 10 Oct: Not having my ears done, Mum & Dad's pressies come first. This morning I got my heater fixed at last for fish tank. Then I got about 6lb of chestnuts with EC. Stayed in after & saw Butch Cassidy & Sundance Kid.

Tue 12 Oct: I'm going down field at 5.00 tonight. Instead of typing & OP I'm doing CSE jog & O' [Level] French. Tonight I went to Mums & then to library. Got a book on sharks, early man & Loch Ness Monster. Then had cider & watched TV.

The True Diaries of a 1970's Teenager: 1976

Wed 13 Oct: Tonight when I got home I went to see a man who sells bikes. He's got a great one for £10. I've got £4.00. Went to see Mum on bikes with RG & Helen. Went down field. Then saw Graham.

Thur 14 Oct: Got £2.50. 7.00 ATV, Survival. Typing an OP all morning. Was late got there at 9.30. Didn't go down field, went to Centaurs. Saw Julie there. Everybody liked my dress. Slept at Mums tonight.

Fri 15 Oct: Andy's 8.00. Had day off cos Joe was ill & I had to look after him. Came home at 7.00 went babysitting. Sold rabbit for £1.50 today. Got home from Andy's at 12 o'clock, went to Scar's ½ hour, came in.

Sat 16 Oct: Cleared house up today then me & June got some chestnuts from near motorway. Got back at 7.00, saw Scarlett. I could have gone to a disco with her but I had to babysit for Andy. Got home at 12.00.

Sun 17 Oct: Got £4.70 for bike. Got today mixed up. The 17th is really the 10th & vice versa. Got up, cleaned shed out. Scarlett came for me. We went down field. Misty was shod. Then I went on tractor & moved some firewood for kids. I had a ride on Blue.

Karen Francis

Scarlett went on Jet. After I had my tea at Scarlett's. Came home & she came to our house.

Mon 18 Oct: *Was late for school again. Tonight I am going down field at 5.00. I've been taken off OP & typing course at school. Hooray! Got a leather coat today & a talking catfish! Then had chips.*

Tue 19 Oct: *Andy 8.00. Went down field. Julie came up got home watched TV & went babysitting for 2 hr. A girl bought my roller skates today. Sally had her nose bit by a ferret.*

Thur 21 Oct: *Tonight I had ears pierced & then went to Mums. After, I went to school disco. Came home at 9.30 because they sent us back (someone let fire extinguisher off). Then saw musical film.*

Sat 23 Oct: *This morning I cleared up & then went down town & did the shopping. Bought a pair of silver earrings like Lyn's £1.75. Then watched 100th Generation Game & went babysitting. On Monday Fred [hamster] escaped & we thought Willie had eaten him but he was behind the fire.*

The True Diaries of a 1970's Teenager: 1976

Sun 24 Oct: *On Sunday I ordered two LPs out of Carol's catalogue. Arab stud fee= 25 guineas. My fish have got white spot. Today I went to kennels on bikes, on way back we talked to a woman who had a lovely Arab stallion & foal. I might have a foal out of him. Tonight I stayed in & listened to Top 20 on radio.*

Mon 25 Oct: *We've got the week off, Hooray! Stayed in all day. RG & Tina Parker stayed at our house. We played games. Tonight I went to RGs house, bought Mastermind & watched film, had chips.*

Tue 26 Oct: *EC came for me & we played Mastermind, chess & jumpy all day in our house. I got dressed at three o'clock & tonight we went to her house & played Masterpiece with Craig. Then we saw TV & I bought a dead rabbit off Craig 75p.*

Wed 27 Oct: *This morning our Helen went spud bashing* [potato picking] *at Clays. She got 75p. I'm going tomorrow. Today I went to EC house. Me & Craig & Emma played Masterpiece. Then later we went outside* [suspicious..]. *Tonight I saw Scarlett for ½ hr.*

Karen Francis

Thur 28 Oct: Number 1 – Pussycat, Mississippi. 1wks- ears. Went spud bashing, got £1.80. We were going to get over £2.00 but it chucked it down with rain so we had to pack in. We were drenched (me, EC & RG) & we were all sludged up (I think my shoes are ruined). Tonight saw Top of Pops & a musical Thoroughly Modern Millie.

Fri 29 Oct: Dad's birthday. Went spud bashing again. This time I put some wellies on (Sally's)- but we came home cos of rain. Today I made Dad a cake then saw EC. Went to her house for a couple of hrs, came home had tea then went to ECs again. We played Masterpiece. Tonight RG came & then I saw a film about witchcraft.

Sat 30 Oct: Had a new green cardigan. I put £2 towards it. Then Helen went shopping & I watched wrestling. Then I saw Demetrius and the Gladiators on TV. Then I had some tuffees [sic] & saw a good French film on TV. Helen slept at Mums tonight & Dad went to pub- not to sleep! After the film I saw Les Dawson on Parkinson & a thing about cowboys. Woke up at one o'clock today.

Sun 31 Oct: LP's should come this week. Julie is selling Blue Boy. Woke up at 10.45. It's EC Bday today. Saw EC after I had dug tomato plants up. Then I went down field & we all went & fetched Julie's hay from farm. Had ride back on trailer. Then had a ride on Blue. Tonight went to EC for an hour, had some cake wrapped in toilet roll.

Mon 1 Nov: School again- boo. Tonight went to welfare disco with Kaz S, Nat. etc. Bill was there (my new heart throb). Slept at Mums tonight. Came back from disco with Kim C. & Julie W. We just missed Budgie having a scrap.

Tue 2 Nov: Started nail piccy today for Mum's birthday. Then saw TV & went to Halloween disco with Scarlett Delaney at school. The hot dogs were best things there (it was chronic). Jezz Chandler was freaking out (that was funny). Got in & went to bed.

Wed 3 Nov: Tonight I finished my picture for Mum. It's called The Lovers. I went babysitting at Scarlett's from 4.00-5.00 then saw James Bond film on TV- Goldfinger. Today Lyn & Shaz told Bill I fancied him (blush, blush).

Thur 4 Nov: Mum's birthday. Number 1- Pussycat, Mississippi. Mum is getting her present tomorrow when she comes up. Tonight I made a bonfire for Joe-Jo then I made some toffee & saw Top of the Pops- Tavares were on. Then saw the Thursday musical, Carmen Jones.

Fri 5 Nov: Bonfire Night. Tonight I made a bonfire for Joe. Mum & Joe came up & we lit fire (Emma & Theresa came as well). We had some toffee & hot dogs, then we went a walk up Misk & then went to EC's house. We made more toffee. It was rock hard. Then I came in at 11.30 & went to bed at 12.00.

Sat 6 Nov: Woke up at 1.00 so did Helen! We cleaned up & had our dinner when Dad came home then watched Tele all afternoon. At 8.00 I went babysitting at Andy's. Got home at 12.00, saw some of The Prisoner & went to bed.

Sun 7 Nov: The murder film was good - The House on Greenapple Road. Got up at 9.15, didn't go anywhere today. After dinner I saw Scarlett. Came in, saw Sally, came in, went to pub, then Christine came & put my earrings in then I saw film.

The True Diaries of a 1970's Teenager: 1976

Mon 8 Nov: *Today I went bowling with school. It's a laugh cos we have to wear funny shoes. Tonight at 6.45 I went to welfare disco. Lyn & June told Bill I wanted to go out with him. He said he will when he packs Jo in.*

Tue 9 Nov: *Tonight I went straight down town after school. Took library books back, saw Bill. I felt stupid. Tonight got a luvly Starsky pic out Jackie then stood on street & saw Stan, June & Gary Lilly. Then saw Les Dawson -on tele not on street!*

Wed 10 Nov: *Helen slept at Mums again. Tonight my Abba LP came. I listened to it & then went to Scarlett's. Made some toffee, then listened to my Abba LP again. Then saw a program on TV & went to bed.*

Thur 11 Nov: *I hope LPs come this week. Tonight I had my tea & went to Mums & played my LP. Her TV broke down, so it was a real bore. I went to her next door neighbours & saw Singing in the Rain- Gene Kelly*

Fri 12 Nov: *Tonight I went to pet shop & bought a long-haired hamster. Then my Carpenters LP came* so I played it. Scarlett came round & we saw Beasts & a suspense film. My hamster is luvly. I don't know what to call him yet -Dusty?

Sat 13 Nov: In morning I stayed in & then saw Scarlett for ½ hour. Went to ECs but she wasn't in so I sat & waited in the house with Craig & her dad. Then I took Dusty to their house & played till 8.00. We had great fun, Jack put lemonade down Emma's back. Then I went babysitting. Mike Randall comes back. No he don't, he comes back at Christmas.

Sun 14 Nov: Number 1 - If you leave me now, Chicago. Got up at 1.00, went to shop & then I cleaned up a bit. After dinner I saw a film on our TV. Then I saw Walton's dad. Went to Mum's, I had a bath & saw The Killing of Sister George -Beryl Reid film.

Mon 15 Nov: Didn't wake up till 12.30 so obviously I had morning off. Tonight I went to library at 5.30 then I nipped to Mum's & then went to Welfare with Karen, Nat, Mandy etc. Didn't see Bill but Jo S was there. Lesley is giving me a hamster.

Tue 16 Nov: After school I went to Lesley's house. She gave me a lovely golden hamster & cage. Her dad brought me home. Then I went to EC & we went in her house & played Funky Music & The Flasher on her record player. Then specky Daniels was on the street. Craig's mates told her he fancied her & she believes them. Today Mark Gun asked me to go out with him.

Wed 17 Nov: Today my ear has gone sore & it is weeping. It looks like I've got to buy some gold sleepers. Went to Mums tonight but didn't stay the night. I just collected my record & my books. Went for sleepers but didn't have enough money. Came in after talking to Karen Wyng then I played records & read books. Went to library on way home.

Thur 18 Nov: Miss World. Film was Rose Marie. 4 wks ears. Scarlett went to Kev's party. After school I saw EC. Then I went to shop & then gave my fish to Sally's. After I went back to EC. Craig had gone out. Came in at 9.00 & saw Miss World - Miss Jamaica won- I predicted it. Then I fed my hamsters & saw some of the musical film.

Fri 19 Nov: I went down field after school with Scarlett & Jed. Then I went for EC & we went in her kitchen. Then Garby came for Craig. We talked to them & then at 8.00 I went babysitting at Andy's. Saw film.

Sat 20 Nov: At 11.30 I went down town with Emma, saw Lyn, June & Maz. Then we bought Funky Music by Wild Cherry. Saw EC this afternoon. Tonight went back to Andy's & when I got back I put my silver earrings in.

Sun 21 Nov: Got up at 2.00, went to ECs. After dinner we watched TV then came to our house. We started a string piccy each at her house. Then her family went to Nabb & I was also on my own so I stayed at her house till 11.00. We did some tying & dying & played records. Also tonight we were curling our hair with electric tongs, mine looked dead nice.

Mon 22 Nov: Before school I washed my hair. After school I had a bath & washed my hair again. I got all dressed up becos [sic] Bill has fell out with Jo & he said he might go out with me when he does - but the swine wasn't there!!

Tue 23 Nov: Had morning off cos I'm not very well - I've got a cold & yesterday in school I fell off the trampoline on my head. Went in afternoon to get my maths books cos it's exam tomorrow. Tonite Scarlett came around & helped me with maths & Biol.

Wed 24 Nov: After school I went down field with Jed. Then I came in & watched TV. Dad went to Mums but came back at 9.00. He was in a bad mood. He hit my ear & made it sore.

Thur 25 Nov: After school I went down field with Jed & Scarlett down town in lorry. I saw Harvey (Craig's friend) I said hey up. It was funny because we were talking about him & Bill & then he walked up. Tonight went down town with Lyn, Len, June & Maggie.

Fri 26 Nov: Tonite I saw Carolyn's purebred Arab colt. It's a beauty. Then I went to EC till 8.00. I played chess with Craig & Jack. I lost. Then I went to Andy's.

Sat 27 Nov: This morning I went down town & did shopping, got back & saw Scarlett. We saw Jason & Argonauts on TV. Went babysitting till twelve but went to Scarlett's till 2.00 am, got in & went to bed at 3.30.

Sun 28 Nov: Got up at 10.00 & went down field. We went to see a little black pony. Then I got back at 3.00

& had nosh. This afternoon I saw EC. I stayed at her house till 10.00.

Mon 29 Nov: [all highlighted] *I'm having a horse!! It's called Rocky, black 13hh. Dad said I can have it. It's £40. All I've got to do is get the money.*

Tue 30 Nov: *After school I went to Mums with Scarlett. Stayed for 1 hr & then we went to the man's house who owns Rocky he said it's £50 but he's going to save it for me. Thank god.*

Wed 1 Dec: *Had day off to look after Helen. She was ill. I did the bedrooms & tonight I went to ECs. We took Brandy to vet & saw Alsatian being put down. Later Scarlett came round. Washed my hair.*

Thur 2 Dec: *Went down field after school then went to EC. Stella passed her driving test today. She was in a bad mood. Saw T.O.P.S & came in.*

Sun 5 Dec: *Got up at 10.30 went down field, did jobs, came back for dinner & went back down. Scarlett went to Leeds to see Michael R. This afternoon I saw Rocky. Got back, I've decided to have a go training Flicka.*

The True Diaries of a 1970's Teenager: 1976

Mon 6 Dec: *Tonight I had a date with Bill S. Lyn & Gribby came out with us. We went to Bulwell on bus & came back. Got in at 10.30.*

Tue 7 Dec: *Went out with Bill again at 7.00. Lyn & Gribby came out. We went to the PP. I didn't have anything. Then me & Bill went to bus stop (I stayed at Mum's).*

Wed 8 Dec: *Uncle Bill's Bday. Saw Bill at 7.00. I go out with him. Joanne is giving me filthy looks at school. Tonight we went to Centaurs with Lyn & Gribby then me & Bill went a walk.*

Thurs 9 Dec: *Went down field then Scarlett came & we saw Funny Face musical. Bill went out to Kung Fu so I didn't see him. Went to bed at 11.00. I was tired.*

Sat 11 Dec: *Got up at 12.00. Helen bought me Flasher. Then I saw Scarlett & went down town & got some presents. Went to Andy's, Bill came.*

Sun 12 Dec: *Mike Randall was home on Friday & Aiden Randall sprained his foot. On Weds Helen broke her toe. Went down field at 8.30. Had dinner &*

stayed in all afternoon. Helen is at Mums. Tonight I went babysitting with Bill, Lyn & Gribby. Got in at 12.00. Dad went mad.

Wed 15 Dec: Jed's birthday. Met Bill at 7.00 on market. Went to Scar's house till 11 then came in & went to bed. Helen broke her toe.

Thur 16 Dec: Tonight I saw Mum. Bill went to Kung Fu. Saw Gribby on way home. EC was at our house, we had some pop. Then saw musical -Carousel. It made me cry.

Fri 17 Dec: Last day today. Didn't go this afternoon, went down town with Lyn, Grib & Bill. Tonight I went babysitting with Scarlett at Andy's house.

Sun 19 Dec: What a day. Went down field but everything went wrong. S'afto I saw Railway Children & tonight I saw EC & then went babysitting with Lyn, Gribby & Bill.

Mon 20 Dec: Today I saw EC. In afternoon we went to her house. After din Craig & Emma came to hear my Queen LP, then went to her house till 12.30. It was great fun.

The True Diaries of a 1970's Teenager: 1976

Tue 21 Dec: *This morning went down town, got Sabbotage for Bill. Then went to our house with EC, JA & Helen. Sold Floppy [my rabbit] for £1.50 then went to Bill's at 6-9. Saw Scar, MR. [Sabbotage was the sixth studio album by English rock band Black Sabbath, released on 28 July 1975].*

Wed 22 Dec: *Centaurs disco. KS Bday. Had bath, went to Bill's at 11.30 till three. Then saw Scarlett & at 7.30 went to Centaurs special disco with KS, DB & NW. It was good.*

Thur 23 Dec: *Helen & Joe are at Mums, Dad at work so I am on my own. Got up at 1.00 went to shop. Saw film then went down field. Then added our Christmas food up - 45 pounds worth.*

Fri 24 Dec: *Christmas Eve. Went down town with EC & her mum. Bought Stop Me. At 1.00 I saw Bill, Gribby & Lyn in Music Box. Went babysitting tonight, Andy gave me a present.*

Sun 25 Dec: *[no entry – 3 stars ***]*

Karen Francis

Sat 26 Dec: *Next year's diary is going to be a big one with a lock & key [should be interesting..]. Hendo's party. Had hangover today, saw TV & went to EC house tonight. I was s'posed to go to a party but I was too ill. CC & Harvey & EC came round.*

Mon 27 Dec: *EC came at 12. We went to her house at 1.30. Saw Call of the Wild -good film about a dog. Then came to our house* [crossed out].

Tue 28 Dec: *Welfare. Shaz & Lyn's party. Went to Welfare with Lyn, Bill & Gribby. Got in at 11. Slept at Mums, had chips. Missed Queen on TV.*

Hucknall Miner's Welfare held large discos in the Welbeck Suite (there are some good slideshows by Pixelthree on YouTube). Following the miners' strike of 1984-85, Hucknall's No. 2 'Bottom Pit' closed in 1986, ending 125 years of deep mining in Hucknall, together with a way of life for many in the town.

Wed 29 Dec: *Went down Notts with Lyn, Bill & Gribby. Got another Queen LP. Got in went to EC till 10, played LP.*

The True Diaries of a 1970's Teenager: 1976

Fri 31 Dec: *EC came at 10.00. We went a long walk to Beauvale Priory & got bottles. Then I played Queen LP. Then I forgot to fill the rest in. What an ending to a diary!*

Postscript

My 1975 and 1976 diary entries show that, in keeping with the time, I was an immature, innocent 15 year-old with a focus on rabbits, horses and eating lots of chips! Many entries made me laugh out loud as I transcribed them, reminding me somewhat of Sue Townsend's character, Adrian Mole (aged 13 ¾). In hindsight, it is also poignant knowing that both of my parents would be gone within the next seven years, changing my life irrevocably.

I am now looking forward to transcribing my much bigger 1977 diary that is easier to read and has the lock on it (as long as I've not crossed out all the juicy bits again!). 1977 was the year that I turned Sweet 16, left school and got my first job (as a pump attendant), at the Esso petrol station, before going on to art college. I hope that next year's diary entries will reveal more about my likes and loves, and my ongoing journey to adulthood and independence in a small Midlands pit town.

The True Diaries of a 1970's Teenager: 1976

Links

https://discovery.nationalarchives.gov.uk/details/r/C6090862

http://www.blackkalendar.nl/c/8917/Derek%20Lawrence%20Scott

https://www.youtube.com/watch?v=YUaI47SUlLI

http://hucknallparishchurch.org.uk/hucknall-collieries/

https://blog.britishnewspaperarchive.co.uk/2024/04/22/hucknall-pit-closure/

https://en.wikipedia.org/wiki/Nadia_Com%C4%83neci

https://www.uk-charts.co.uk/index.php/charts/1970-s/197-1976#google_vignette

https://www.penguin.co.uk/series/ADRMOL/adrian-mole

Printed in Great Britain
by Amazon

56062559R10047